Light At The End Of The Tunnel

'To' Danyelle

Thank you 'Danny' for all
of your support.

anthony
6/13/12

LIGHT AT THE END OF THE TUNNEL

How I Achieved Financial Freedom in Five Steps

Anthony Willingham

authorHOUSE®

AuthorHouse™
1663 Liberty Drive
Bloomington, IN 47403
www.authorhouse.com
Phone: 1-800-839-8640

First published by AuthorHouse 1/28/2011

ISBN: 978-1-4520-0547-8 (sc)
ISBN: 978-1-4520-0548-5 (hc)
ISBN: 978-1-4520-0549-2 (e)

Library of Congress Control Number: 2010917409

Printed in the United States of America

This book is printed on acid-free paper.

Certain stock imagery © Thinkstock.

Preface

I was not prepared to take on the tasks of fixing my brother's mind and spirit when he came to live with me.

Anthony was clueless to what was really going on. I saw that he had a decent salary, but he didn't know what to do with it. He believed that carrying high credit card balances and borrowing money were the way to get ahead in life.

Anthony was paying triple for everything. If my memory serves me correctly one of his credit card's interest rate was around 32%. I thought that was illegal, but after finding out that he had allowed matters to go so far they were allowed to apply their new default rate.

The climb out of the mess he made was hard for him. I was giving him a lot of new financial concepts, some of which he would not accept at first.

I use to ask him questions like "why are you paying ATM fees to get your own money?" He would answer, "it's just $1.50" or "why are you allowing credit card companies to charge you a fee to pay your bills by phone?" He would just shrug his shoulders.

Throughout the time he stayed with me I would ask him similar questions constantly, so I could show him that he had to restructure his finances and his way of thinking.

Andre Willingham

Notes

Dedication

I would like to thank God for all the things he has done for me. I would also like to thank my mother and father, who have always been there for me no matter what; my twin brother Andre; my sisters Terri and Brenda; my twin daughters Taylor and Tiffany; and Ursula, for having my daughters. Lee, thanks for inspiring me to write this book. Carolyn, even if nobody else knows anything about me, I know you do. Thanks to my girl Linda for being insightful and a great friend and to all my brothers and sisters who work the hardest beats behind the walls. I would also like to thank Rev. Dr. Marvin J Bentley, for letting my brother and I conduct our first financial seminar; Latica, for the helpful ideas; My barber Mark, for introducing me to Authorhouse and to my new family at AuthorHouse and all the people who knew my financial situation and stayed by my side. Finally, my thanks go to President Barack Obama.

This book is dedicated to all those who are looking for the light at the end of the tunnel.

Running on Sinking Sand

I got my money sweet to me like honey
Gonna buy that thing, so I can ring
Like the church bell, don't know it'll bring me to hell
Feel the heat burning my hand
Quickly running on sinking sand

—Anthony Willingham

Contents

Chapter 1   Going Into the Tunnel   3

Chapter 2   Step 1: Believe in Yourself   11

    Change Your Thinking   13
    Being Discouraged   14

Chapter 3   Step 2: Get Organized   17

    Analyze Your Paycheck   20
    Make a Budget   21
    Track Your Spending   24
    Tips That Can Save You Money   27

Chapter 4   Step 3: Call Your Creditors   29

    Dealing with Commercial Creditors   30
    Dealing with the IRS   33
    Debt Consolidation   33

Chapter 5   Step 4: Pay Yourself First   35

Chapter 6   Step 5: Open a Savings Account   39

    Investing   40

Chapter 7   Coming Out of the Tunnel   43

    A Word of Encouragement   43

Introduction

Dealing with the burden of debt can be a crushing experience for anyone. The hopelessness, despair, and pain can feel more real than the debt itself. I know because I've been there—caught up in out-of-control credit card debt, which is the worst because of the ballooning interest rates and late fees.

It can seem as though no matter how much money you make, you can never give enough to your creditors to see any progress. The more you pay, the less the debt goes down. Compound that by four, five, six, or more credit cards, and your situation can look hopeless.

And let's not forget there are living expenses that must be met: the rent or mortgage, utilities, food, the list goes on. On top of everything else, you might have a loved one (living with you or not) who wants you to pay for the things he or she desires. Last (but not least!) you may have children, and we all know how expensive they can be.

Well, I have good news: there is light at the end of the tunnel. Just five steps can get you out of debt or at least help you manage your debt. That was all I wanted—to have some kind of control over my finances.

I know this probably sounds too good to be true. Just five steps? Well, it *is* true. I didn't say five *easy* steps. There will be some effort on your part, but it's nothing you can't do.

Once you apply these steps you should start to feel the life, empowerment, and happiness you deserve come back to you.

These are the steps:

Step 1: Believe in Yourself

Step 2: Get Organized

Step 3: Call Your Creditors

Step 4: Pay Yourself First

Step 5: Open a Savings Account

I want you to have a starting point from where you are now—financially, emotionally, and spiritually—so you can begin your journey to financial freedom.

PART ONE: MY STORY

Chapter 1

Going Into the Tunnel

I have been working for the state of New York since I was seventeen years old, and I have had hundreds of thousands of dollars slip through my hands for twenty-seven years. For all of that time I was foolish in the handling of money. I used to max out my credit cards on clothes, shoes, jewelry and stereo equipment. Then I would pay the cards down just so I could max them out again.

I did it so I could get a thrill. Spending all that money made me feel good. I call those kinds of purchases *comfort buys*. I thought buying things (with my credit card because I had already spent all my cash) would get rid of some of the things that were bothering me. It made me feel good for a little while, but the feeling never lasted long.

At the age of forty-two I was faced with insurmountable debt. I also owed the IRS thousands of dollars, and I had nowhere to turn.

The debt collectors began calling me at home and at work day and night. Sometimes I wouldn't answer the telephone at all. Other times, when I did answer, I would disguise my voice and tell them that I wasn't there. What kind of silly mess is that? As a corrections officer, I excelled at work. But as a grown man with children and a wife I was playing games—telling complete strangers on the phone that I wasn't there.

The sick part about it was that I really started to believe that I wasn't there, because if I kept telling my creditors that, then maybe I wouldn't have to pay back the debt.

It may sound crazy, but I did it. And as I continued to practice taking myself out of the equation of life, my family began to believe it too. I wasn't there.

When I did speak to the creditors, I used to pretend to take down the 1-800 numbers they gave me so I could get back to them, by scribbling the numbers in the air with my index finger. For a long time I thought I was fooling my creditors by doing this. I eventually found out I was the fool.

They started to write me letters, some of them threatening to sue me for the total balance due. The amounts were so high I used to look at the letters and ask myself over and over again, "What the hell did I buy? And why can't I show anything for it?"

I used to dread going to the mailbox. When I opened it, I would only take out the pieces of mail I wanted. The thin white envelopes with unknown return addresses would stay inside.

All my financial resources were being tapped out—just like me. I was working three jobs, and I was exhausted.

I used to gamble and borrow money from friends, family, and myself. Almost every year I took out thousands of dollars in retirement loans. After a while I couldn't borrow any more. I even took a loan for five thousand dollars from my 457 deferred compensation plan because I was three months behind on the rent.

I owed the IRS over fifteen thousand dollars in back taxes. The credit card companies wanted all their money back, and I still had to pay child support. It was killing me because all of this was happening at once.

All my schemes to make extra money, including working overtime, came to a screeching halt. I was left to face the debt head-on like a grown-up and pay it back. But I really didn't know how I could do it with the money I was making.

How was I to take the money that I made and reasonably spread it over all my bills and living expenses? Where was I supposed to start? Who could help me? I was too embarrassed to ask for help.

If I started to pay, and my plan didn't work, then what? Up to that point I had been a failure with my finances so I felt I couldn't trust myself to get out of my mess.

Fear began to grip me even more tightly, which made me do nothing. That was the worst thing I could have done. My inaction made the balances balloon. When I realized that hiding from the problem was not my best option I began to beat myself up viciously for not addressing the issue earlier.

During all of this, my wife left me and took our twin daughters with her. I started to feel all alone and depressed. Thoughts of suicide raced through my mind. Believe it or not those thoughts were comforting to me at the time because I was watching my whole world crumble right before my eyes and there was nothing I could do.

I had never had thoughts like those before, but my debts were so big they overwhelmed me. In my mind they took the shape of a monster trying to crush me. I couldn't take it anymore. I was expected to be the provider of the household, but I was failing again.

Now, don't think I was crazy. I wasn't. I was desperate and looking for a way out. For the first time in my life, when I heard stories on TV of men and women who had killed themselves over their finances, I understood why. I listened to the reporters, families, and friends describe those people. They were for the most part hard-working, decent folks, but somewhere down the road they had made a wrong turn (or a few wrong turns) and gotten off at the wrong exit. They were looking for some light at the end of the tunnel, as was I.

I knew my thoughts of suicide were bad, so at my most desperate hour, I dropped to my knees in my dark bedroom, clutching my hands as tightly as I could. In a trembling and weak voice, I pleaded to God to help me out of my situation, and I promised that I would do whatever it took to get out.

I quickly began to feel that everything was going to be alright. I didn't know how, but I held on to that belief like my life depended on it—and it did.

I started to listen to the financial talking heads on television, but they weren't talking to me. I read a few financial books, but I couldn't understand how any of what I was reading applied to me and my life.

In another desperate move, because I had to borrow more money *again*, I called my twin brother, Andre, whom I knew had the money and a better way of living.

Six years earlier Andre had retired from his job as a New York City corrections officer, with houses, nice clothes, jewelry, and a Mercedes-Benz. He had traveled around the world. Shoot, to me it looked like he had everything!

During that conversation we both agreed it would be best for me to move in with him. On June 27, 2006, a day after our birthday, I arrived at his house with six big cardboard boxes, plastic garbage bags, and a broken spirit.

The first thing my brother said to me in the hallway was that, if I didn't do exactly what he said, he would throw me out. I didn't care about his threat. He stressed to me that I had to change the way I was thinking. My thinking had put me in my awful situation. I didn't want to hear that either, but I slowly let it sink into my hard head.

The second thing he did was ask me to assess the damages by gathering and organizing all of my bills. The third thing he established was the rent: three hundred dollars a month. Lastly he saw to it that I gave my wife money for our twin daughters.

After we were done talking and tallying up everything he said, "Anthony, I can help you." I looked him in his eyes and told him that I didn't believe him. As we sat at his antique dining table, he looked me in my face and guaranteed me that at least all of my credit card debts would be paid off by September. I just looked back at him and thought, "There's no way in hell."

Andre began the process of teaching me what he had already known for years. He had told me about the right way to deal with one's finances before—but I hadn't been willing to listen. Now I was completely his. My mind, heart, and soul were opening up to hear all that he wanted to impart to me. What he didn't know was that I was going to keep the promise I had made with God.

These five steps were the building blocks to my personal success with money:

Step 1: Believe in Yourself

Step 2: Get Organized

Step 3: Call Your Creditors

Step 4: Pay Yourself First

Step 5: Open a Savings Account

I am not rich yet, but I am on the road to financial freedom, and completing the first step (believing in myself) was so enriching to me. For the very first time in my life I began seeing the light at the end of the tunnel.

Before we continue I must say that nothing on these pages from this point on can guarantee you the same results that I achieved. I make no promises that you will get out of debt—that's up to you.

PART TWO: THE FIVE STEPS TO FINANCIAL FREEDOM

Chapter 2
Step 1: Believe in Yourself

I have to talk about this topic first, because I have found that when you don't believe in something, you won't do it.

If you don't believe exercise is good for the body for example then you won't ever work out. When you don't see instant results after the first workout and you're sore the next day, you might decide to quit. If you were told it would take time to slim down and build muscle and that the soreness would eventually go away, only recurring every now and then, you might keep going.

Well, that's what this book is all about: giving yourself time to exercise your finances. I want you to believe that you have time.

When I was younger, I never thought I would make it to my forties. While I was growing up in the Woodside projects, I thought I was nothing. But now I place a high value on my own life. I can look forward to making good on my debts and enjoying the rest of my life.

I have to get you to believe my story, that what I told you thus far works when applied, and that just about anyone can do it—but only if you believe.

While Andre was showing me what to do I didn't believe it would work either. Remember, he had told me many times before about this process; but even at my lowest point I was still too stubborn to accept the time-tested laws governing the use of money.

In a few short weeks I observed some small results, which made me start to believe and want more of what I was feeling and seeing. I made an extra effort to read more of the finance magazines that I couldn't understand before and to apply the things my brother had taught me. I turned off the TV and got off the couch (which I slept on) so I could get out of the miserable situation I had put myself in.

It is easy to look at your circumstances and think that all is lost. You may think it's hopeless. When you keep telling yourself that you don't have anything, a feeling of despair can quickly come over you.

If this is your thought pattern, I want you to stop thinking this way. Just stop. I want to be abundantly clear that you have a lot of good and positive things going for you.

I learned that lesson when my brother was looking at my W-2 form from the year before. He saw my annual income and seemed impressed with the amount. He said to me, "Anthony, with the money you make, I can't understand why you are in debt."

Up until that point he hadn't known how much money I made. His comment was a blow to my manhood, but at that very moment I had to see the good in it. I was grateful to have a salary I could work with to eliminate my credit card debt and to manage the other debts.

As we talked I started to feel good that I had worked for ten years in good standing as a corrections officer. Although all my bills were unorganized, I could be glad that I had still kept them.

So what I want you to do is focus on your strengths. I don't care how insignificant you may think they are. Just sit by yourself and write down some good things about yourself. I did, and it made me feel good.

I had to encourage myself by looking in the mirror, which I hardly ever did before then. Every day I would say, "You can do this, Anthony. You've *got* to do this." Most important, I had to believe what I had asked God for.

Change Your Thinking

I want you to change your thinking about how you handle money. It was one of the first things Andre said to me when I moved in. It was important that I got this right because the rest of the things he showed me would have meant nothing otherwise.

I could not have applied any of the rules he taught me until he helped me unlock my mind. The more my thinking changed, the more quickly I could climb out of the tunnel I was in. The way he unlocked my mind was to first make me look at myself. (Remember, I promised God that I would do anything to get out of debt.)

I realized I wasn't so nice to the people in my life. I was rude and disrespectful to some of them, lashing out instead of addressing the real issues within myself. Honestly, I did not know what those issues were at the time. There was a bigger issue at hand, and I had to control it just like I had to get a handle on my finances.

I bought so many things to make me feel good—so I wouldn't have to look at what was really bothering me. I used to purchase stereo components, and the speakers always had to be the biggest and the most thunderous. At the time I felt I deserved that stuff. My thinking was, "I worked hard all week. So what if I want to buy some stereo equipment for myself?" The problem was that I was buying those things almost every week.

One day while I was reading my Bible in my brother's living room, God revealed to me what was hurting me: I thought I was ugly and a failure. When I was made to take a hard look at myself, I did some real soul searching.

Once that was over, I felt a whole lot better. I cleared my head and only allowed positive thoughts into my mind.

When negative thoughts like "You're never going to get out of this" came into my head, I hurriedly conquered them with positive thoughts like "Yes, I can." I rebuffed the negative words people said to me, even when it meant I had to disconnect myself from some family members and friends. I thought it was going to be hard, but it became easy when I reminded myself that I was fighting for my financial life.

Don't be afraid to do some soul searching. In my case, some of this even took place when I was sorting my debts (See chapter 3, Step 2: Get Organized).

Without unlocking my mind and changing my way of thinking, I could not have gotten out of debt. I realize that now. It was easy for me because I wanted to get out. I hope you do too.

Being Discouraged

I had been incredibly discouraged when I was in debt, but when I started to put things in order and save my money, I actually became discouraged again. Some of you might begin to feel the same way, but I don't want this to happen to you too.

It seemed that I was getting on this plan just to pay bills and eliminate my debts. But that's not all of what's supposed to happen. I want you to be able to sleep peacefully at night (no matter what you're laying on) and wake up feeling strong, looking forward to the future, and being joyful—not afraid anymore.

I encourage you to make small celebrations for yourself.

When I eliminated my credit card debt in September of 2006 just as Andre had predicted, he took me to Lord and Taylor, a department store. We went all the way to the back, where the clearance rack was. I bought a nice shirt and two pairs of linen pants at a great price.

The best part about it was that I bought everything with cash. I walked out of the store with a bag of designer clothes *and with no regrets*. That was a first. The experience only encouraged me to continue doing what I was doing.

I began to block out those thoughts that said, "Man, this isn't going to work." I had to keep telling myself that it *would* work—that I was going to live my life debt-free.

The feeling of being enslaved to my debts was no joke. So when I heard the first set of chains fall off and hit the ground, I did whatever it took to get the rest of them off me.

Don't be discouraged. Keep doing what you are doing—it will pay off.

Summary

1. Your results are not going to be instant. Give it time.

2. Encourage yourself.

3. Change the way you think about money.

.

Chapter 3

Step 2: Get Organized

This, my friends, is the next step toward the light. Without this step, it is *impossible* to achieve your financial goals.

Just like me, you have made a mess, and now you are going to have to clean it up.

Remember your parents telling you to clean up your room? Well, that's what this is: cleaning up your room. You are going to have to do some corner cleaning. No, you can't throw your stuff under the bed or in the closet to just make the room *look* clean. You are going to have to get down and dirty.

Please, don't let this alarm you. I highly recommend that you organize everything by yourself because I want you to actually see the financial mess you have created. This was therapeutic for me—not right away, of course, but as time went on.

When I was putting those papers together, the ones from under my bed (I had dusty shoeboxes filled with bills, receipts, and old papers), it made me realize how much of a mess I really had made. I had closed envelopes from the bill collectors in the kitchen drawer, which I had stuffed closed. Department store bags filled with papers hid out in the back of my closet.

It made me feel good to finally get the mess organized. Please don't forget to look in the mailbox. I know you stopped checking, because I did.

I had placed all my bills in a black weekender bag when I moved in with Andre. When I arrived, he told me to sort them. Slowly I started to pick up all these pieces of paper with numbers and words on them and tried to make sense of them but it was very trying.

First of all, I couldn't focus on what I was supposed to do, because I was missing my family so much.

I must not have been doing such a good job because eventually Andre came over, grabbed the bag, and dumped the entire contents on the floor. I was pissed, but he yelled at me to get all the papers in order. I thought he was being mean. I later understood the value of getting organized when we called the creditors (See chapter 4, Step 3: Calling Your Creditors)

I decided not to let my anger get in the way of me getting out of debt. I got as comfortable as I could, sitting on the floor with my legs spread in a V and my back against the couch, sorting through all my bills and drinking a glass of juice. It was morning when I started and well after midnight when I finished.

I had thought Andre was being mean, but that wasn't the case at all. I had to learn that when you make things chaotic for yourself you have to be the one to bring order.

The other good thing I got out of that experience was a good five hours of peaceful rest, which I was not getting before, because I was up all night thinking about how I was going to get out of debt.

It made me feel good to start putting things in order. I spent the next morning doing more of the same, except it wasn't quite as hard.

It took me about two weeks to fully organize everything. It took so long because I didn't have my papers in order, and everything was scattered everywhere.

Once I got all my bills together I had to find a good file box to put them in. I picked my favorite kind, an accordion file with pre-labeled tabs so I could neatly put everything away and have it handy at my fingertips. You can use whatever you want.

Generally, they are not that expensive—ten to fifteen dollars, depending on where you go. Sometimes the stores have two-for-one sales, so bring a friend and help them get organized as well!

If you are doing this with your husband, wife, or significant other, I highly recommend separate file folders. If you share a bill with someone else, get together to figure out who is responsible for what and go from there. If it starts an argument, then just get back to organizing the bills that you do agree upon. Be aware that your biggest fight is up ahead with your creditors, not with each other. You are going to need your strength, so with your favorite music playing, start organizing those papers. And remember this: credit card companies, the IRS, and debt collectors are organized—so you should be too.

Now that you have gathered all of your bills and neatly put them together in a way that is understandable to you, I want you to take the most current credit card statement (or the most current one you can find) and look for the lowest balance.

For example, if you have five credit card statements and the lowest balance out of all of them is five hundred dollars, then that's the one you will start with first. You will tackle the higher-balance cards later.

Now you might be asking yourself: *Why the lowest balance first? Aren't you supposed to start with the card with the highest interest rate?* Yes, you could, but there are two reasons I want you to do it this way:

1. I want you to accomplish a small task with very little effort.

2. I want you to start to believe that you can do this.

When Andre told me to do it this way, I couldn't see the logic either. But when I started to complete those smaller tasks I began feeling a lot better about myself and the whole situation. It kind of made me feel empowered. Although he didn't take the time to explain to me why we were doing it that way, he knew he couldn't give me too much to tackle at one time. Andre knew that he was still dealing with a wounded animal.

Analyze Your Paycheck

The next thing I want you to do is take your paycheck or any check that you receive on a regular basis and analyze it for inaccuracies and unnecessary deductions.

The way Andre and I accomplished this was by looking at all of my before- and after-tax deductions: in my case, union dues, health, life, and disability insurance premiums.

He was able to reduce some after-tax deductions like my disability and life insurance premiums by twenty dollars each pay period. He felt that I was carrying too much insurance at the time and asked me whether I actually needed all of it. I gave it some thought and realized I really didn't.

We called the insurance company, and they allowed me to lower my premiums and continue to get the coverage I needed (Step 3: Calling Your Creditors, in chapter 4).

Andre had helped me find forty dollars a month. That was a lot of money to me and enough to help me pay down my debt even faster.

After finding this extra money, Andre sat down at his kitchen table and recalculated the budget he and I had created earlier. (I will discuss budgets in detail later in the book.)

With the new numbers in hand he asked me, "Do you have any money on you?" I said, "Yes, five dollars." He replied, "Good, because everyone has been paid for this pay period."

I'll never forget the awesome feeling of relief that washed over me as I stood there and heard those words. I looked down at him and began to cry. Andre asked me, "Are you crying?" I told him that my situation had been killing me and that it had been years since I'd had all my bills paid with money left over. Surprisingly, the creditors stopped calling me, too.

That was the day I began to see the light at the end of the tunnel.

You might also benefit from taking a look at other tax deductions. Please check with a tax professional to see which options are best for you.

Make a Budget

Now you might be thinking, "What about me? I'm not going to keep paying bills all my life and get nothing out of it." You are right. I haven't forgotten about you.

When I was going through this, I was getting a little annoyed too, until Andre structured a budget for me. I was taken aback at first. I had thought budgets were for businesses. Believe it or not, my budget turned out to be one of my best friends.

I disrespected this friend at first, and he made me pay for my disrespect. Once I learned not to do that again, in hard times I was able to lean on him, and like a pillar he held me up.

Brothers and sisters, the meaning of the word *budget* is the amount of money that is available for, required for, or assigned to a particular purpose.

You see, this kept me out of trouble, provided me with the things I needed, gave me a sense of responsibility, and put some extra money in my pocket to do whatever I wanted with.

Trust your budget, and constantly review it so you are always on track. I do, and I feel great about it. Now that I use one and make it part of my life I wonder how I ever lived without it.

It is simple to set up a budget for yourself. Write out all your expenses (bills) and then allocate your income to your bills. It works best when you're honest.

When Andre was helping me to write out my budget, there were some numbers that I didn't want to see, but in the long run it helped me out a lot.

Here's an example:

Monthly Income: $1,000.00

- Savings account deposit $5.00 (See chapter 4, Step 4: Pay Yourself First)

- Rent $550.00

- Credit cards $30.00 (minimum payment for two)

- Cell phone $50.00

- Cable $80.00

- Food $150.00

- Entertainment $50.00

Total $915.00

This simple example illustrates how a budget is formulated. You can plug in your own numbers. The $85.00 left over would go in your pocket. By all means, if you can pay a little more toward your bills, please do.

I must admit, getting on a budget was an incentive for me to eliminate my debts. The more I paid off, the more money I had left over to pay myself first (See chapter 4, Step 4: Pay Yourself First) and have extra money to buy some of the things I wanted.

I was also ecstatic when the child support for my oldest son, which I had been paying for twenty years, ended in July of 2006. It enabled me to save more and also pay down more of my bills.

When I started to write out my debts, set up my pay-back dates, and map out strategies to pay back the people I owed, it felt good.

JUNE						
M	T	W	T	F	S	S
	1 (Rent)	2	3	4	5	6
7	8	9	10 (Credit card#1)	11	12 (Food Shopping)	13
14	15 (Credit card#2)	16	17	18 (Cell Phone)	19	20
21	22	23 (Cable)	24	25	26	27 (Movies)
28 (Savings account deposit)	29	30	31			

This simple example illustrates how a calendar is used. Write in the bills according to their due dates. The miscellaneous bills, such as food shopping and the movies just pick a day that you will spend the budgeted amount of money.

I began to walk to the local supermarket with my coupons in hand to buy food. I sought the best prices for my toiletries and bought them in bulk whenever possible. For entertainment I went down to the bookstore to sit down and read. I took long walks in the park, too, and the exercise didn't hurt me either. By all means, be creative.

I used to laugh at people who read books all the time and stayed in. I never thought in a million years that I would be doing some of the same things. One of the best parts about it was that it felt great!

Sometimes, a sense of vulnerability would sweep over me during this period. I kept thinking about what I was going to do for money until I got paid again. I wanted to use a credit card so badly, but I put a plan of action in place to get me through: I remembered the ducking and hiding I used to do, the sleepless nights, and those intimidating phone calls.

I don't want you to think that you can't go to the movies, hit the town with your friends, or go to your favorite restaurant. But you will have to put those events on pause until things get better.

Now I use a calendar to figure out what I'm going to do with my money in the future. I write down the due dates for *all* my bills.

Initially that was hard for me. I didn't want to see my future. I believed in looking only at the moment. Remember when I said I never thought I would make it to my forties? Well, as part of that, I used to think, "Planning for the future? Are you kidding? Never!"

This is definitely a process, so take your time. It makes no sense to cheat. Have fun with this, invent new things, laugh—it will get better.

Track Your Spending

I know, I know ... you can't live off what you make now, right?

Well, that's not necessarily true. I used to think the same way, but I'm going to show you what Andre threw at me to help me change my thinking.

This, my friend, is the key that unlocks the door to financial freedom. I'm going to show you that you do have enough money. I have some questions for you, and please be honest when you answer.

1. Do you buy coffee, tea, or your favorite beverage outside of your home on a daily basis?

2. Do you buy lottery tickets or scratch-off games on a daily or weekly basis?

3. Do you treat yourself to your favorite footwear, jewelry, or clothing items often?

Remember, I'm trying to change the way you think. I'm going to show you how you've been putting money everywhere except where it belongs—in your wallet or purse.

In this example I'm going to pick on the people who play the lottery and all those gambling games, but be aware that this illustration applies to everyone.

Suppose you buy one lottery ticket for one dollar every day for one year. How much money would you have spent? This is easy: $365.

1 lottery ticket @ $1.00 × 365 days = $365.00

If you saved one dollar a day for the same amount of time, you would have $365 instead of slowly giving it to someone else.

Imagine ten thousand people purchasing $365 in lottery tickets in a year from one neighborhood store. That business would wind up making $3,650,000.

10,000 people × $365.00 = $3,650,000.00

I'm being kind when I suggest that it is only one lottery ticket a day. We know that it is much more than that. I know because I used to play. If that illustration doesn't upset you, then add up all the other needless stuff you buy.

Take, for example, buying a cup of coffee every day for one workweek at three dollars a pop. When you add that up, it totals fifteen dollars. In a month all those cups of coffee cost sixty dollars.

1 cup of coffee @ $3.00 × 5 days (one workweek) = $15.00

$15.00 × 4 weeks (one month) = $60.00

Even the lunch you buy every day (which can run you about ten dollars a day) adds up. See for yourself.

1 lunch order @ $10.00 x 5 days = $50.00

$50.00 x 4 weeks =$200.00

There were many other things I used to purchase on a daily basis that slowly sucked my money out of my pocket, including cigarettes, beer, candy, movies, music, and even check-cashing fees.

I hope you understand what I'm saying to you. I really want you to get this; if you don't, the rest of this book will be useless. Using the same formula, plug in your own numbers for the things you buy in any given week. When I did, it made me sick to see the money I was wasting.

So, you see, you have the money; the problem is that you are spending it on things that you don't need to buy. Start making your lunch at home and bringing it to work with you. Make your own coffee, and invest in a good insulated cup to take with you on your commute.

So, what am I trying to say here? Track your spending. Don't buy unnecessary things. And if you can make it or do it yourself, set aside the time to do so. Go ahead. What else do have to lose?

Tips That Can Save You Money

1. Avoid ATM fees

2. Check all receipts for errors

3. Buy energy-efficient appliances

4. Bring your lunch to work

5. Eliminate premium cable stations

6. Shop with a list

7. Eliminate unnecessary cell phone features

8. Eat at home instead of dining out

9. Use coupons

10. Wash your own car

Summary

1. Gather all of your bills.

2. Sort all of your bills.

3. File all of your bills.

4. Start paying down the lowest balance first. (remember continue paying your other creditors)

5. Write out a budget and stick to it.

6. Track your spending.

7. Analyze your paycheck or income source statement for inaccuracies and unnecessary deductions.

Chapter 4

Step 3: Call Your Creditors

The next step is to call your creditors. I must admit you don't *have* to call them, but that was the way we did it so we could attack the debt head on.

There are two reasons why you should contact your creditors. The first reason is to find out how much you actually owe. The second reason is to see if you can have some of the fees waived or reduced.

It doesn't make any difference how you contact them—by telephone, e-mail, regular mail, or smoke signals—just get it done.

I was afraid to hear what I owed. To be honest I didn't want to know. Now this may sound funny, but you'd be surprised to find out that you might not owe as much as you think. When I called one of my creditors I was shocked to hear that the amount wasn't as high as I had dreaded it was.

One credit card company told me that I owed a really high amount, a crazy number. It was so high because they had tacked on a bunch of fees and charges. My new default interest rate was jacked up to the highest level possible.

Whatever you do, don't call these people by yourself. I wanted you to sort your bills by yourself because it was your clutter. I also wanted you to see what kind of mess you had created. But for the creditor calls, I recommend that you rely on someone whom you totally trust and are comfortable with, a person who has his or her act together (preferably a person who has his or her finances in order). You'll need someone there to guide and support you, especially when he or she hears something that's not right. I had my brother with me, and I was glad he was there.

Please be careful when you call; these creditors are not your friends, and they have a few tricks up their sleeves. One trick in particular is that when they get you to agree to pay a specific amount, it turns out that the money is only enough to cover the late fees and will not go toward the principal.

Be aware that you are still a wounded animal and the people you are dealing with are highly trained, skilled, organized, relentless hunters. They will stop at nothing to get their money back, so you and your partner have to be the same way. When you get through with this part, I want you to feel like you are king of the jungle.

Dealing with Commercial Creditors

Before you call, make sure you have all your bills handy and organized. Always write down the names of the people you talk to as well as the times and dates that you call. Jot down all important information that is discussed like the amounts owed, account numbers, and any charges that you are disputing, and be sure to let them know when you don't understand something.

It's a good idea to have access to a computer so you can go to their Web site. There you will be able to see what they see and e-mail them, if necessary. It's also a good Idea to have a calculator, a calendar, and a fax machine nearby, if available.

All these things came in handy when Andre and I called, especially when we were put on hold and ended up speaking to somebody completely different a few minutes later. When we were on hold we took that time to review my account for any discrepancies and re-strategize our approach based on that information.

We also wrote out questions before each call, such as:

1. How much do I actually owe?

2. What can I do to eliminate some of these fees and late charges?

3. How can I restructure a payment plan that I can afford?

4. Have you reported this charge as being delinquent?

5. What steps can I take to dispute a charge?

Always be clear when you talk to your creditors. Tell them you are restructuring your finances. That's what I told them. Don't assume they know what you want. Lastly, be assertive yet polite; and above all, be honest. You are already seen as a credit risk, don't be a liar too—not a good look.

If you aren't having success with the first person you talk to, then kindly ask for a supervisor. Your goal is to get those fees and extra charges reduced or eliminated. Sometimes the first representative doesn't have the authority to make that change; insist on speaking with someone who does.

You'll find that at times they are going to be aggressive. At first they will sound pleasant and helpful, but when you don't follow their script, watch out! They will tell you things like "You know, you owe us a lot of money" or "This debt has been long overdue." But always reiterate that you called them to settle the debt reasonably with a comfortable payment plan that you can afford.

When you set the payments up, make it so that it is easy for you. It is a good idea to have your calculator and calendar handy for this.

Sometimes they may ask for what Andre and I used to call "good-faith money," a small amount of money that is promised to your creditor to get negotiations going. Use this tactic *only* if you have extra money to give and always use it to get what *you* want first, such as having the current balance lowered.

Once things seem to be to your satisfaction, agree upon the structured payments. Get this and any other promises put in writing *before you send any money.* Ask them to fax or email the agreement to you. Once you confirm the terms of the deal send the money and stick to it.

I do not recommend allowing creditors to go into your checking account. (That's when you authorize a bank, financial institution, or in this case your creditors to debit a specific amount of money directly from your bank account.) I know it is convenient, but doing it this way usually incurs a fee.

Pay them either by online bill pay through your own bank or by mail. Doing it this way gets you in the habit of paying your bills, and the creditors can start trusting you again. You also don't have to pay a fee for this.

Please do not be dismayed. Not all creditors are alike, and some will work with you as long as you are willing to make a commitment to sticking to whatever agreement is made. I found this out with a few of the creditors that I spoke to.

Keep in mind that this process could take hours, but whatever you do, never, ever hang up—no matter how frustrated you get.

We would do only one creditor a day, and we would usually start in the morning. If we were done by noon, I would celebrate with a peanut butter and jelly sandwich and a glass of milk, my favorite.

Continue to do this until all of your creditors have been addressed. This is not going to happen overnight, so don't expect it to. Take your time, and remember this: you slowly put yourself into debt, so you'll have to slowly climb out of it.

If you are calling a collection agency this step is still the same; they want money, too.

Dealing with the IRS

As you can imagine, dealing with the IRS was a lot different, but when I did call them, they let me know what my repayment options were.

I had to give up all my banking and personal information, and they gave me several different monthly payment amounts to choose from to be spread out over a certain amount of time.

I picked the installment agreement that I was comfortable with. They let me know my recourse if I didn't agree with the amount that they said I owed.

My experience with them was not as bad as I thought it would be. They answered all my questions and were courteous to me.

I do recommend that you get a tax professional or visit www.irs.gov, which is what my brother recommended to me. He admitted that he couldn't handle the IRS. It will be worth it; you don't want to mess with Uncle Sam.

Debt Consolidation

I won't say too much on this topic, as I have no personal experience with debt consolidation companies, but I do feel that something should be said.

I have heard positive and negative things about them. When I found out exactly how they worked, I could see how they could bring relief to someone; but what I also noticed with the people that used them was that they went right back to their foolish ways of dealing with money.

It was sad to see people go back into debt—sometimes even more debt than they had originally. It's a quick fix for a stemming problem that could get worse over time.

I've told you before that my brother impressed upon me the importance of changing the way I was thinking. That was the best way for me to get out of debt and stay out. Why have somebody else do something for you that you can do yourself?

When I was in my twenties, I filed for bankruptcy. It was a quick fix, but I continued to disrespect money, and I paid for it by going right back into debt years later.

Summary

1. Have all your organized bills available to deal with your creditors.

2. Write out all of your questions before calling your creditors.

3. Be patient. *Never* hang up during a call.

4. Have a computer, calculator, calendar, and fax machine available, if possible.

5. Get a tax professional to help you deal with the Internal Revenue Service.

Chapter 5

Step 4: Pay Yourself First

Every time you get money, I don't care how little, always pay yourself first. When Andre told me about this, I thought he was a complete fool. How could he tell me to pay myself first when he could clearly see that I didn't have enough money to pay my bills?

He made it simple by reminding me that I was taking the time to pay those other people, so why couldn't I pay myself? The concept did make some sense when he put it that way, but I was quite curious to know *how* it worked. In fact it was simple to do, and I had already started it—and didn't even know it.

I want to keep this simple. Years earlier I had enrolled in what is called a deferred compensation plan, otherwise known as a 457 plan, named for section 457 of the Internal Revenue Code (IRC). This is how it works: You defer pre-tax dollars into an investment account that you control. The investment portfolios can be very conservative, meaning you risk a little of your money and receive a small return over time, or lose a little. Or you can be very aggressive by risking a lot of your money so you either receive a large return over time or lose a large sum.

That's all I want to say about that; hopefully you get the idea. At the time my brother and I were talking about this, I was deferring 6 percent of my income.

Some of you might have heard of this in another way as a 401k or 403b, also named for sections of the IRC. The whole idea behind this concept is to sock away at least 10 percent of your income until you retire, after which, you can live off the money comfortably.

I used to think that my pension and social security would be enough, but I was wrong. If you retire at age sixty-two and you live until you are seventy-two, wouldn't you like to have enough money in your pocket to do the things you want to do instead of being broke in your old age?

Now I know this concept might not sit well with some of you because I am talking about the future. Remember I used to think like you, too. I used to recite all the clichés, like "I might die tomorrow" and "I'm not going to deny myself anything." Well, my friends, don't end up thinking like me and deny yourselves financial freedom.

If you can't fathom putting that much money away, then by all means, start small by putting away just 3 percent, like I did.

When I started to knock off those creditors one by one, my thinking also changed, and I began to feel it was better to invest in my future. Let me tell you, it's a great feeling.

So go to the human resources administrator at your job or at a financial institution that you trust and look into this. Don't be afraid. You can do it.

I went from 6 percent to 8 percent and then to 12 percent in a year—and guess what? It didn't even hurt. More money was available to me because of my new financial skills so I could make it happen.

One thing I don't want you to do is to contribute dollar amounts. You make out better when you contribute percentages, because you sock away more of what you make. Take advantage of the fact that when you receive a bonus, a raise, or overtime. Your nest egg just gets fatter and fatter.

Take the time to discuss your options over the telephone, by e-mail, or in person with the people who know best. You can also visit the Web site pertaining to your state. (For example, check out the New York site: www.nysdcp.com.)

When you set this up, have it automated. I had it deducted from my paycheck automatically, so I never felt like the money was missing;

but whenever I saw it in my quarterly statements, I would smile from ear to ear and say, "Wow! I did that?"

Summary

1. Check with your bank or human resources administrator to open an IRA (Individual Retirement Account.)

2. Contribute at least 10 percent of your income to your 401k, 403b, or 457. If that's not feasible, start with one percent.

3. Have the deductions debited automatically. (That is when you authorize a financial institution to withdraw money from your account on a specific date each month.)

Chapter 6
Step 5: Open a Savings Account

Now that you have organized your bills, set up the repayment plans with your creditors, learned how to track your spending, and automated contributing 10 percent of your income into an investment portfolio, you're ready to open a savings account.

If you don't have one already or the one you do have doesn't have any money in it because you're afraid someone might garnish your account, then I recommend following the previous steps first before opening one up.

Andre didn't know that some years earlier I had opened up a savings account. The problem with that account was that I frequently dipped into it so I could bail myself out of financial trouble. No matter, though—my brother was impressed that I even had one!

I'm going to tell you how I did it; it was so simple. I had gotten an invitation from ING Direct in the mail, so I filled out an application, which was very straightforward, and set up fourteen-dollar biweekly deposits into the account by authorizing them to transfer funds from my checking account into my new savings account.

The beautiful part about it was that there was no minimum dollar amount to deposit. It grew quickly, and the neat part about it was that as a bonus they deposited twenty-five bucks into the account just for opening it.

Over time all those fourteen-dollar deposits grew; at that time the annual percentage yield (APY) was around five percent, not bad for a man who was headed toward financial destruction.

They are almost entirely an online-only bank, with just a few brick-and-mortar café locations. You can visit them at www.ingdirect.com.

You can also contact them via phone or mail to complete all of your transactions.

Another thing I really love about them is their security. I find it hard sometimes to get into my own account! I don't mind, though; if it's hard for me to get in, then it might be harder for the thieves.

No matter which bank you choose, just pick one and let compound interest do the rest.

Investing

It is difficult to start investing when you don't know how to invest. I'm going to tell you what I did. It was simple, and in a month or so, I saw the results.

One of the simplest ways for me to begin was by buying I bonds. Oddly enough, I was introduced to these things by accident.

I went to work one day and saw a lady with her wares set up on a table from the National Bond and Trust Company (www.nbtco. com). She explained to me the different denominations of I bonds, the lowest being fifty dollars, with the face of Helen Keller on it. It was easy to set up automatic payroll deductions, which authorized NBT to deduct money directly from my paycheck in order for me to pay for them.

Remember, I like automation, and so should you. It is convenient, and there are no fees involved to use the service.

After setting up the payroll deductions, I also added a life insurance policy, which is optional. In the event that I died, my daughters would still receive a bond a month for the next ten years (the bonds were originally for their education).

If I didn't die by the time the girls needed the money, then the insurance premiums that I paid out would come to Papa. A nice little savings account is being built up on the side as it's accruing interest. Not bad for a financially distraught dad.

What is so special about I bonds? Well, they are guaranteed by the government, so they are pretty safe. You can cash them in after one year if you want to, but I wouldn't. Look at these bonds as long-term investments. You can visit www.treasurydirect.gov on May 1 and November 1 to check out the interest rates and other information.

The kicker for me was that they adjust with inflation. That means the bonds don't shrink in value over time like some other investments and currencies. In other words, the fifty dollars you spend today will continue to have its staying power ten, twenty, and thirty years from now. You can also get these bonds and other high-yield investments from a bank that you trust.

I strongly suggest that you also talk to a financial advisor or someone at your bank about other high-yield investment accounts.

Summary

1. Contribute small dollar amounts to a bank account on a consistent basis.

2. Find alternative investments that yield safe returns.

3. Always protect your investments. Look for guarantee-backed investments.

Chapter 7
Coming Out of the Tunnel

This journey had its ups and downs. I created all my ups and prepared for my downs. But what a feeling I had inside when I was able to go to my family reunion, a cruise to the Bahamas!

When it was over, I left knowing I owed nothing. We had a wonderful time. It was the first time my brother and I cruised together, and we took a lot of pictures. When I saw myself in those photos, it was the first time in years I really saw a happy person. I was also happy when I was able to see my daughters on the weekends.

I began to plan other events, big ones and small ones. The biggest one was when I came up with the first and last month's rent for my own apartment.

Andre was very happy for me, and I thanked him for what he had done for me. He replied, "I didn't do anything—you did."

A Word of Encouragement

My journey was not easy. I had to overcome a lot of things. But giving up is not an option to consider while going through this. Whatever it is that keeps you going, focus on it and seek the light at the end of the tunnel.

For I, the Lord your God, will hold your right hand,
Saying to you, "Fear not, I will help you."

—Isaiah 41:13 (NKJV)

Light At The End Of The Tunnel

how I achieved financial freedom in five steps

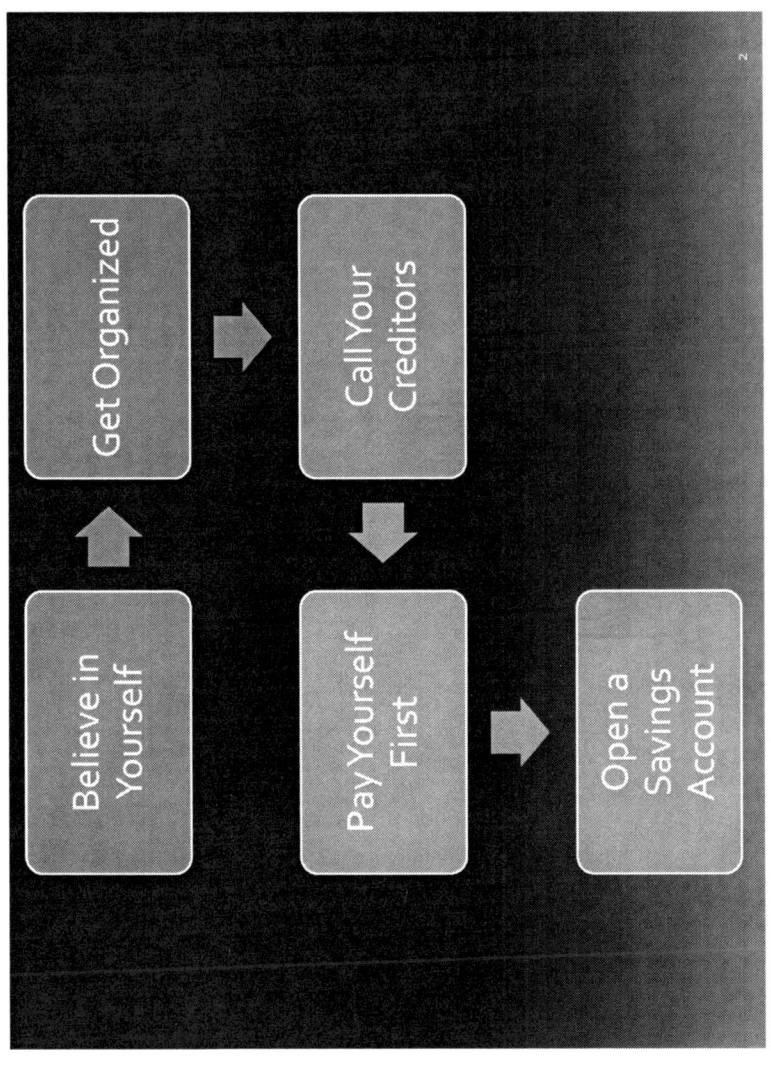

VALUE

The value of this book is to show you how to regain your financial freedom in five (5) steps without stressing yourself any more than you have to. Why you need to take control of your finances now and to make you feel EMPOWERED over all your financial decisions.

QUESTION?
OBJECTIVE ONE

Name the first thing you must do to start Believing in Yourself?

Answer:
Change Your Thinking

OBJECTIVE ONE

The three(3) steps in order for you to Believe in Yourself are:

- Change your thinking
- Apply the rules governing your finances
- Do some real soul searching

OBJECTIVE ONE

this is not easy but …

- DON'T BE DISCOURAGED
- GIVE IT TIME
- LEARN FROM YOUR MISTAKES
- STAY FOCUSED
- MAKE SMALL GOALS
- NEVER GIVE UP

OBJECTIVE TWO

The five(5) steps in specific order for organizing your debts are:

1. Gather
2. Sort
3. Make a budget
4. Set up a payment plan
5. Track your spending

OBJECTIVE TWO

1. **GATHER** all your bills. Go in all the places that you have stuffed your bills: the shoe box under the bed, the bag in the closet, a drawer that you can hardly close or open. Please, don't forget to look in the mail box, they have the most current balances.

OBJECTIVE TWO

2. SORT all your bills in any way you want, so that it can be easily retrieved. You can use;

☐ An accordion file

☐ Any type of bin or box

☐ A folder

☐ Anything that helps you organize your bills, be creative

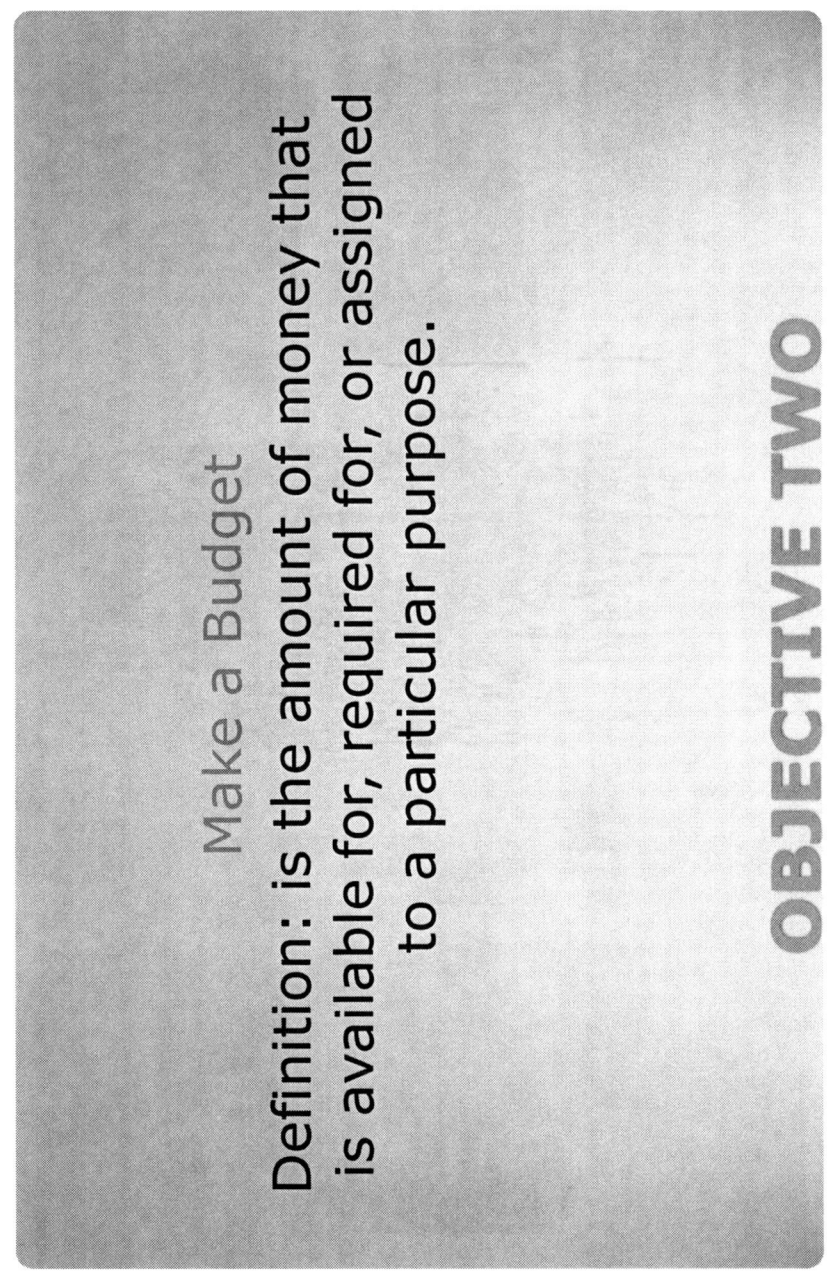

Make a Budget

Definition: is the amount of money that is available for, required for, or assigned to a particular purpose.

OBJECTIVE TWO

OBJECTIVE TWO

Example of a budget

Monthly Income: $1,000.00

1) Savings account deposit $5.00
2) Rent $550.00
3) Credit cards $30.00(min. payment for two)
4) Cell phone $50.00
5) Cable $80.00
6) Food $150.00
7) Entertainment $50.00

Total $915.00

OBJECTIVE TWO

3. <u>*SET UP a PAYMENT PLAN*</u> and stick to it.

Start with the **lowest** balance, even if the interest rate is high.

i. I want you to get a sense of accomplishment.

ii. I want you to have more money to tackle the next highest balance.

iii. I want you to keep paying the other creditors the minimum monthly balance.

OBJECTIVE TWO
Ways To Find Money

Track Your Spending

Examples:

✓ 1 lottery ticket @ $1.00 x 365 days= $365.00

✓ 1 cup of coffee@ $3.00 x 5 days= $15.00

✓ 1cup of coffee@ $3.00 x 365 days= $ 1095

✓ 1 breakfast order @$ 5.00 x 5 days = $25

✓ 1 lunch order @$10.00 x 5 days=$50.00

OBJECTIVE TWO
WAYS TO FIND MONEY

Analyze your paycheck or any income you receive on a regular basis.

✗ Check the before and after tax deductions such as:

✗ Insurance premiums.

✗ Union dues.

✗ Any other inaccuracies.

OBJECTIVE TWO
Ten Ways To Save Money

1) Avoid ATM fess
2) Check *all* receipts for errors
3) Buy energy-efficient appliances
4) Bring your lunch to work
5) Eliminate premium cable stations
6) Shop with a list
7) Eliminate unnecessary cell phone features
8) Eat at home instead of dining out
9) Use coupons
10) Wash your own car

OBJECTIVE THREE

THE FIVE(5) ITEMS you will need before you contact your creditors are as follows:

- ✓ A notebook or writing pad
- ✓ A calendar
- ✓ A fax machine (if available)
- ✓ A computer (if available)
- ✓ A calculator

OBJECTIVE THREE

When you contact your creditors always get the names of the people you speak to, the time, the date and what was discussed. Your goals are:

I.   To find out what the ***actual*** balance is as of the date you're calling.

II. To have the late and/or over limit fees waived or eliminated.

III. To use the calendar to set up payback dates.

IV. To get an agreement in writing before you make your first payment. That's why you may need a fax machine

OBJECTIVE FOUR

The two(2) steps in specific order you must do to Pay Yourself First are:

i. Contribute at *least* ten percent(10%) of your income to an IRA (individual retirement account) or a 401k on a consistent basis. (if possible start with 1%)

ii. When contributing have it automated

OBJECTIVE FIVE

Four things you should do to Open a Savings Account.

1. Pick a bank or financial institution that you trust.

2. Make the deposits automatic.

3. Put away small amounts consistently.

4. Have a goal in mind for the money.

SEEK THE LIGHT!

About the Author

Anthony Willingham was born in Queens, New York. He was educated in the public and Lutheran school systems. After graduating from Martin Luther High School, he started working at Bernard Fineson Developmental Center, a state facility for the mentally challenged. In 1996 he started his career as a New York State corrections officer. While working at various correctional facilities, Anthony took advantage of all the training that was available to him. As part of this training, he received his certification from the Municipal Police Training Council as a general topics instructor, which allowed him to teach Department of Correctional Services policies and procedures to state employees. He also spent time at the World Trade Center disaster site as a member of the Corrections Emergency Response Team. He currently lives in New York and is the proud father of four children: Christopher, Demitrious, and twin girls Taylor and Tiffany.

About the Book

Take a journey with twin brothers Andre and Anthony Willingham as they triumph over debt. Anthony, who has done everything wrong with money—and then some—finds himself deep in credit card debt and owing the IRS thousands of dollars. Follow the steps that Andre taught Anthony to help him overcome his depression and sleepless nights—and finally find peace of mind.

http://awillingham64.blogspot.com

My email address: awillingham64@yahoo.com

Notes

Notes

Notes

Notes

Notes

Notes

CPSIA information can be obtained at www.ICGtesting.com
Printed in the USA
BVOW031956310512

291513BV00001B/69/P

9 781452 005478